Learning English

Using Punctuation and Capitalization

TEXTBOOK WITH ANSWER SECTION

BY
LOUISE M. EBNER

Learning English

Using Punctuation and Capitalization

TEXTBOOK WITH ANSWER SECTION

BY
LOUISE M. EBNER

John 20:31
"But these are written, that ye might believe that Jesus is the Christ, the Son of God; and that believing ye might have life through his name."

AMG
PUBLISHERS
Chattanooga, TN 37422

LEARNING ENGLISH: USING PUNCTUATION AND CAPITALIZATION

©1998 by Louise M. Ebner
Published by AMG Publishers
All Rights Reserved.

ISBN 0-89957-804-7

Library of Congress Catalog Card Number: 98-87265

Printed in the United States of America
03 02 01 00   –B– 6 5 4 3 2

INTRODUCTION

The Bible is God-inspired. Every word in the original manuscripts of the canonical books of the Old and New Testaments was selected by God and given to the writer to give to us with the preservation of his own individual style. That is a miracle.

Since the Bible is such a miraculous book, why is it not used in classrooms as a perfect language instrument? The world is poorer for not having used the Bible also for grammatical and systematical purposes.

God has given Mrs. Louise Ebner, a veteran educator, the vision to use God's Word, the Word not only for salvation and inspiration, but also for linguistic instruction.

Of what use is knowing grammar if one's life is not in conformity with the Creator's designs?

It is our hope that as grammar is learned through God's Word, that Word will sink into the heart while the mind is instructed.

Spiros Zodhiates, Th.D.
President, AMG International

TABLE OF CONTENTS

LEARNING ENGLISH:
USING PUNCTUATION AND CAPITALIZATION

INTRODUCTION

LEARNING ABOUT PUNCTUATION

DidyouknowthatinearlyEuropeanwritingthelettersrancontinuouslyinlinesCanyouimaginet
ryingtoreadastoryinwhichnowordsareseparatedfromoneanotherHowwouldyouknowwh
ensentencesbeganorended

Did you have difficulty in reading the above paragraph? Probably you did because it lacked punctuation and spacing. Now read the paragraph with punctuation marks.

Did you know that in early European writing the letters ran continuously in lines? Can you imagine trying to read a story in which no words are separated from one another? How would you know when sentences began or ended?

As time passed, a regular system of points, signs, and spaces was developed. The system was called punctuation, from the Latin word *punctus,* meaning "a point." Punctuation is necessary to understand the correct meaning of a sentence. For example, read the following sentences from Luke 23:43 and then choose which one is correctly punctuated.

"Verily I say unto thee today, "Thou shalt be with me in paradise.'"

"Verily I say unto thee, 'Today thou shalt be with me in paradise.'"

Should a comma be placed before "Today" or after "Today"? If the first sentence is correct, then Jesus told the criminal next to him that He was speaking to him at the moment, that is, "Today."

In the second sentence the comma is placed before "Today," which means our Lord promised the malefactor that he would be in Paradise during the day.

Correct punctuation is indeed necessary to the meaning of the sentence. Problems of punctuation can arise because writers and publishers do not follow the same style. Some use an **open** style approach which means omitting punctuation unless it is absolutely necessary for clarity. Others use the **close** style of punctuation, which is more formal and follows rules of punctuation. In this book, the rules of close punctuation will be followed.

JUST FOR FUN

Can you write a few sentences in which the placement of a comma changes the meaning of the sentence?

CHAPTER 1

LEARNING ABOUT END MARKS

LESSON 1-A

Recognition of End Marks

A declarative sentence makes a statement. A period follows a declarative sentence.

Examples:

    a. "Fairest Lord Jesus" is a well-known hymn.

    b. Little is known about the origin of the hymn.

An interrogative sentence asks a question. A question mark follows an interrogative sentence.

Examples:

    a. Has the hymn been called the "Crusaders' Hymn"?

    b. Has much research been completed to discover who wrote the hymn?

Note: A question mark may be used within a sentence. If information is doubtful the question mark is placed in parentheses.

Example:

    The tune was first sung in the twelfth century (?).

An imperative sentence expresses a command or a request. A period follows an imperative sentence. If the command is very dynamic, an exclamation point may be used.

Examples:

    a. Read about this song in an encyclopedia.

    b. Find a copy of "Fairest Lord Jesus" in a hymn book.

    c. Do it now!

An exclamatory sentence expresses strong feeling. An exclamation point follows an exclamatory sentence. When the exclamation is not emphatic, a period may be used at the end of the statement.

Examples:

    a. That's a very beautiful song! (emphatic)

    b. O, it rejoices my heart. (not strong)

An elliptical sentence or an expression that has no subject or verb is punctuated as understood.

Examples:

    a. Wonderful work!

    b. Such talent.

EXERCISE 1

Put the correct end punctuation after each sentence. Then tell what kind of a sentence each is.

Example: Popular legends have been told about the hymn. <u>a declarative sentence</u>

1. Was the song sung by children on the Crusades_____

2. What an exhausting trip they made to the Holy Land_____

3. Some believe the hymn was used by the followers of John Huss_____

4. Read about John Huss in an encyclopedia_____

5. Was the hymn first written in Germany_____

6. Some say the song was first used in America in the early 1800s_____

7. Did Richard Storrs Willis popularize the hymn_____

8. He also composed "It Came Upon a Midnight Clear"_____

9. How creative_____

10. O, I wish I could write a song_____

EXERCISE 2

Write two declarative sentences.

_____

_____

EXERCISE 3

Write two interrogative sentences.

_____

_____

EXERCISE 4

Write two imperative sentences.

_____

_____

EXERCISE 5

Write two exclamatory sentences.

_____

_____

EXERCISE 6

Write two thoughts or elliptical expressions that should be punctuated as if they were complete sentences.

_____

_____

WATCH OUT!

A common error which many students make in writing is called a "run-on" sentence. The error occurs when two sentences are combined without using a period or some other mark of punctuation (which you will learn later) to separate the sentences.

Example:
Error—I enjoy studying sentence structure I want to be a good writer.
Correct—I enjoy studying sentence structure. I want to be a good writer.

JUST FOR FUN

Obtain a copy of "Fairest Lord Jesus" from a hymn book. List as many characteristics of the Lord Jesus Christ as you can find in the song.

Example:

Ruler of all nature

1. _____

2. _____

3. _____

4. _____

5. _____

CHAPTER 2

LEARNING ABOUT THE PERIOD

LESSON 2-A

A period is placed after a declarative or imperative sentence.

Examples:

    a.   We will now study abbreviations. (Declarative sentence)

    b.   See the previous chapter for an explanation of an imperative sentence. (Imperative sentence)

LESSON 2-B

A period is placed after an abbreviation except in the case of some government agencies and in the metric system. When in doubt, use a dictionary.

Examples:

    a.   Mr., Sr., Dr., U.S., yd.

    b.   TVA, UFO, cm, kg

The U.S. government has specified a two-letter form for names of states when used with zip codes. No period is necessary. Example: NY, TN

NOTE: When the last word in a sentence is abbreviated, only one period is needed.

    Example: The Dead Sea Scrolls contain literature dating from the fourth century B.C.

LESSON 2-C

A period is placed after the initials of a person's name.

Examples:

    a.   John T. Adams

    b.   H. Taylor

LESSON 2-D

A period is used to separate whole numbers and decimals.

Example:

    a. $5.25, 5.8 miles

LESSON 2-E

A period is used in an outline to indicate the division of a subject.

Example:

I.

    A.

        1.

        2.

    B.

        1.

        2.

            a.

            b.

            c.

LESSON 2-F

Three periods, separated by spaces, are used to denote an omission in quoted materials. If the omitted material is at the end of the sentence, four periods are used.

Example:

a. Jesus shall reign wher-e'er the sun does his successive journeys run; His kingdom spread . . . Till moons shall wax and wane. . . .

LESSON 2-G

A period is placed inside parentheses when they enclose a complete sentence.

Example:

Philip P. Bliss , who wrote "I Will Sing of My Redeemer," died in a train accident.
(I do not know the cause of the accident.)

LESSON 2-H

A period is placed outside the parentheses when the enclosed material is not a complete sentence.

Example:

> The hymn was found in his trunk (apparently unharmed).

EXERCISE 1

Place periods and end marks where needed in the following story.

> "O Little Town of Bethlehem" was written by Mr Phillip Brooks in A D 1868
>
> Brooks was born in Boston, MA in 1835 Did he attend Howard University or Boston College
>
> Brooks was a gifted man, a giant in size (6 ft 6 in) as well as in mind Imagine delivering a sermon at the rate of 250 words per minute Wow
>
> "O Little Town of Bethlehem" was written after Brooks returned from a visit to the Holy Land (He must have been moved by that visit)

EXERCISE 2

Match the following abbreviations with the correct meaning. The first one is done for you.

_6_ 1. yd.	1. Anno Domini
___ 2. R.S.V.P.	2. company
___ 3. A.D.	3. Young Men's Christian Association
___ 4. Co.	4. before Christ
___ 5. a.m.	5. European Economic Council
___ 6. SW	6. yard
___ 7. B.C.	7. Doctor of Philosophy
___ 8. YMCA	8. please reply
___ 9. EEC	9. southwest
___ 10. Ph.D.	10. before noon
___ 11. Gov.	11. for example
___ 12. ibid.	12. that is
___ 13. e.g.	13. in the same place
___ 14. i.e.	14. and so forth
___ 15. etc.	15. governor

Note: When using the abbreviation B.C. with a number, the number comes first—43 B.C. With A.D. the number follows the abbreviation—A.D. 432.

EXERCISE 3

Write the name of the state indicated by the following abbreviations. The first one has been done for you.

1. AL   <u>Alabama</u>

2. ME   _____

3. IA   _____

4. MA   _____

5. WA   _____

6. AK   _____

7. AZ   _____

8. WI   _____

9. DE   _____

10. MD   _____

EXERCISE 4

Use your dictionary and write the meaning of the following abbreviations:

1. viz.

2. L.L.D.

3 n.

4. adj.

5. SYN

6. v.t.

7. L.

8. pl.

9. pp.

10. Fr.

JUST FOR FUN

Listed below are eight lessons which we have studied for using the period. See if you can find examples of each from a magazine or newspaper and insert the examples in the proper place. If you cannot find examples, then write your own.

LESSON 1

A perod is placed after a declarative or imperative sentence.

1.

2.

3.

4.

5.

LESSON 2

A period is placed after an abbreviation except in the case of some government agencies and in the metric system. When in doubt, use a dictionary.

1.

2.

3.

4.

5.

LESSON 3

A period is placed after the initials of a person's name.

1.

2.

3.

4.

5.

LESSON 4

A period is used to separate whole numbers and decimals.

1.

2.

3.

4.

5.

LESSON 5

A period is used in an outline to indicate the division of a subject.

1.

2.

3.

4.

5.

LESSON 6

Three periods, separated by spaces, are used to denote an omission in quoted materials. If the omitted material is at the end of the sentence, four periods are used.

1.

2.

3.

4.

5.

LESSON 7

A period is placed inside parentheses when they enclose a complete sentence.

1.

2.

3.

4.

5.

LESSON 8

A period is placed outside the parentheses when the enclosed material is not a complete sentence.

1.

2.

3.

4.

5.

CHAPTER 3

LEARNING ABOUT THE COMMA

A comma is a mark of punctuation needed to indicate a pause and to give a clear understanding of the meaning of a sentence.

LESSON 3-A

A comma is used to separate words, phrases, and clauses in a series. In close punctuation a comma is used before the conjunction. (See pg. 51 in *Learning English with the Bible* for information on conjunctions.)

Examples:

a. Ignatius, Polycarp, and Justin were Christian martyrs in the early days of the Christian church (words in a series).

b. Many other Christians suffered persecution, endured trials, and lost their lives (phrases in a series).

c. Paul was imprisoned, Stephen was killed, and others were persecuted (clauses in a series).

Note: Many authors prefer to use the semicolon instead of a comma to separate independent clauses. See pp. 151-155 in *Learning English with the Bible* for information on clauses.

EXERCISE 1- REVIEW:

Write the 7 coordinating conjunctions. (See lesson 7-B in *Learning English with the Bible*, page 51.)

1._____   5._____

2._____   6._____

3._____   7._____

4._____

EXERCISE 2:

In the following sentences insert commas wherever needed:

1. Was Nero a Roman emperor a Christian martyr or a private citizen?

2. Justin Martyr was captured scourged and beheaded.

3. Other rulers who persecuted Christians were Emperor Decius Emperor Marcus Aurelius and Valerian.

4. Emperor Galerius became violently sick suffered torments requested prayer and finally died.

5. Christians were martyred churches destroyed and Bibles burned.

6. To escape persecutions Christians hid in passageways catacombs and tunnels.

7. As the Christians were martyred they prayed sang and worshipped.

8. Origen Blandina and Irenaeus were also killed.

9. Justin Martyr thanked God for salvation joy and hope.

10. In America Christians are not burned at the stake thrown to wild beasts or put in prison.

LESSON 3-B

A comma is needed to separate two or more adjectives.

Example:

During times of persecution, could you be a strong, brave, and loyal Christian?

Note: The use of commas between adjectives allows the writer some freedom. If the adjectives destroy the relationship between the adjective and noun following it, the comma may be omitted.

Example:

The martyrs were loyal born-again Christians.

LESSON 3-C

No comma is needed if the words in the series are connected by conjunctions such as and, but, or.

Example:

I admire people like Paul and Stephen and John.

EXERCISE 1

Place comma where needed in the following sentences.

1. Three Apostolic Fathers were Clement Ignatius and Polycarp.

2. Do you suppose these men were called Apostolic Fathers because they were taught by the apostles and lived in the second century?

3. The Apostolic Fathers wrote simple thoughtful comments about Jesus Christ.

4. Did you know that Irenaeus and Tertullian and Clement and Origen were called Church Fathers?

5. Our knowledge of the Trinity comes from the hard laborious thoughtful study by the Church Fathers.

6. Have you ever read *Against Heresies* or *Against Celsus* or Justin's *Apology*?

7. Soon creeds canons and organizations developed in the church.

8. Read about the Apostles' Creed the Nicene Creed and the Chalcedon Creed in a church history book.

9. The heresies of the Gnostics and the Montanists prompted the need for a creed.

10. Why was it necessary to develop terms such as "presbyter" "bishop" "diocese" and "episcopal"?

LESSON 3-D

Commas are used to separate cities from states and from the rest of the sentence.

Example:

Cyprian was born in Carthage, North Africa, around 200 A.D.

LESSON 3-E

Commas are used to separate the day from the year. A comma for writing dates is not needed between the month and the year.

Example:

October 24, 1492

October 1492

WATCH OUT!

Another common error which many students make in writing is called a "comma fault." This occurs when two complete sentences are joined together by using a comma rather than a period or a semicolon.

Example:

Wrong: Writing correctly is easy, it only takes time to learn the rules.

Correct: Writing correctly is easy. It only takes time to learn the rules.

TEST ON CHAPTER 3

Place commas and end marks where needed in the following sentences.

1. Abraham probably lived around 2,000 B C

2. Isn't it interesting to learn about the religious political and geographical setting of the Bible

3. God preserved Noah his wife and his family when the flood came

4. How wonderful that God put a rainbow in the heavens and made a covenant to show His love

5. The <u>Great I Am</u> promised to deliver the Israelites from bondage in Egypt and take them to the promised land

6. The Greek translation of the Old Testament was completed around 100 B C

7. It is called the Septuagint (meaning 70 years)

8. Many New Testament writers referred to the Septuagint (It means 70 years)

9. Can you give a definition of the words Pharisees Sadducees and Koran

10. On August 6 A D 70 Roman forces invaded the temple in Jerusalem

JUST FOR FUN

Listed below are five lessons which we have studied for using the comma. See if you can find examples of each from a magazine or newspaper and insert the examples in the proper place. If you cannot find examples, then write your own.

LESSON 1

A comma is used to separate words, phrases, and clauses in a series. In close puntuation a comma is used before the conjunction.

1.

2.

3.

4.

5.

LESSON 2

A comma is needed to separate two or more adjectives.

1.

2.

3.

4.

5.

LESSON 3

No comma is needed if the words in the series are connected by conjunctions such as and, but, or.

1.

2.

3.

4.

5.

LESSON 4

Commas are used to separate cities from states and from the rest of the sentence.

1.

2.

3.

4.

5.

LESSON 5

Commas are used to separate the day from the year. A comma for writing dates is not needed between the month and the year.

1.

2.

3.

4.

5.

EXTRA CREDIT

Write a definition or a fact about each of the following words:

1. The apostle Paul

2. Nero

3. Justin Martyr

4. Polycarp

5. Ignatius

6. Abraham

7. Noah

8. Septuagint

9. Pharisees

10. Sadducees

CHAPTER 4

MORE LEARNING ABOUT THE COMMA

LESSON 4-A

A comma is used to separate *nouns of direct address* from the rest of the sentence. (See Lesson 9-H on pp. 75-76 in *Learning English with the Bible* for further information on nouns of direct address.)

Examples:

    a. **John**, I think you understand that in poetry we find abstract nouns. (John is the noun of direct address.)

    b. Yes, **Mrs. Jones**, I understand. (Mrs. Jones is the noun of direct address.)

EXERCISE 1:

Punctuate the following sentences which contain nouns of direct address. <u>Underline</u> the nouns of direct address and their modifiers.

1. Mr. Server I would like a pepperoni pizza.

2. So would I my friend.

3. Now John eat only a few pieces.

4. "Goosey Goosey Gander whither dost thou wander?"

5. Students have you read *Goodbye Mr. Chips*, a novel by James Hilton?

6. "Now listen my children, and you shall hear of the midnight ride of Paul Revere."

7. "Hence loathed Melancholy of Cerberus and blackest Midnight born." (From "L'Allegro" by John Milton)

8. "Ruin seize thee ruthless King!" (From "The Bard" by Thomas Gray)

9. "Return O holy Dove return." (From "Walking with God" by William Cowper)

10. "Little Lamb God bless thee." (From "The Lamb" by William Blake)

LESSON 4-B

A comma is used to separate an *appositive* or an *appositional phrase* from the rest of the sentence. An *appositive* is a noun or noun phrase which follows a word and denotes or renames the same person, place, or thing. See Lesson 9-G on pp. 73-74 in *Learning English with the Bible* for further information.

Examples:

    a.   Chrysostom, <u>a famous preacher</u>, was banished because of his faithfulness.

    b.   Barbarian tribes, <u>the Huns and the Goths</u>, plundered Rome.

Note: When the appositive is a single word, called a restrictive apposition, a comma is not necessary. (Example: My brother John is an avid reader.)

EXERCISE 1:

Punctuate the following sentences using commas wherever they are needed. **Also**, underline the appositive or the appositional phrase.

1. Three church fathers—Ambrose Jerome and Augustine—played an important role in church history.

2. Jerome another great leader in the church made a Latin translation of the Bible.

3. Jerome's translation of the Bible the Vulgate is still used.

4. Perhaps the greatest of the church fathers Augustine was born in North Africa.

5. Monica Augustine's mother was a Christian.

6. Augustine wrote two very famous works *Confessions* and *The City of God*.

7. Did you know that Simon Stylites lived on top of a pillar a *stylus*?

8. Chrysostom an eloquent preacher was exiled to Pontus and died on the way.

9. Monasticism began in Egypt and monks lived in large houses monasteries.

10. The Word of God the Bible proves that practices like prayers for the dead and a belief in purgatory are unscriptural.

EXERCISE 2:

Write 5 sentences using appositives or appositional phrases.

1.

2.

3.

4.

5

LESSON 4-C

A comma is used to separate *parenthetical expressions* from the rest of the sentence. (See lesson 8B - pp. 55-56 in *Learning English with the Bible* for further information on parenthetical expressions.)

Examples:

    a. **In my opinion**, the culture in America is becoming less Christian.

    b. That is, **of course,** because Christians fail to defend the faith.

EXERCISE 1:

Write five examples of parenthetical expressions.

1. _____

2. _____

3. _____

4. _____

5. _____

EXERCISE 2:

Underline the parenthetical expressions in the following exercises and place commas where they are needed.

1. Evolution of course is not a science.

2. Evolution is basically a religious philosophy and therefore not a science.

3. To be sure Bible students must believe that God created the heavens and the earth.

4. The Bible moreover tells us about a reliable account of creation.

5. Furthermore secular humanists oppose Christianity.

6. That means in other words that humanists have replaced Christianity with an anti-Christian religion.

7. When observing fossils for example make certain your answer is consistent with scientific facts.

8. For example look at pictures of fossils and make certain the illustrations are really true.

9. Fossils do however exist.

10. Needless to say much work must be done by students of archaeology.

LESSON 4-D

A comma is used to separate an interjection from the rest of the sentence. (See Lesson 8-A on pg. 55 in *Learning English with the Bible* for further information on interjections.)

Example:

Oh, you mean science has not proven evolution.

EXERCISE 1:

Punctuate and underline the interjections in the following sentences:

1. Well I never believed in evolution.

2. Wow isn't it amazing how we can be deceived?

3. Oh I am so glad that the Bible declares that God is the Creator of heaven and earth.

4. Hurrah for Christian archeologists.

5. Ah that's good news.

LESSON 4-E

Use a comma to separate independent clauses in a compound sentence. Remember, an independent clause is a simple sentence. The comma is placed before the coordinating conjunction.

Example:

I like to learn about things, but I dislike taking tests.

EXERCISE 1:

List seven coordinating conjunctions (If you need further information on coordinating conjunctions, see Lesson 7-B in *Learning English with the Bible* page 51.)

1.

2.

3.

4.

5.

6.

7.

EXERCISE 2:

Place a comma wherever needed in the following sentences. Underline the coordinating conjunctions.

1. Rome was invaded by barbarians in A.D. 432 but Christianity continued to spread.

2. The barbarians were uncivilized yet they had a religion.

3. The story of Clovis is very interesting for he saw a sign of the cross in the sky.

4. Was Clovis a king and was he baptized after his victory?

5. Was St. Patrick a monk or was he an emperor?

6. The Angles and Saxons invaded England and destroyed Christianity for they were heathens.

7. Boniface has been called "the Apostle of Germany" and St. Patrick has been named "the Apostle of Ireland."

8. Why did those men acquire those names and was it right to give them those distinctions?

9. There is more to learn about the spreading of Christianity yet time doesn't allow it.

10. Would you like to write a one-page paper on the extension of Christianity throughout Europe and could you include information on Boniface, Gregory the Great, and Augustine?

LESSON 4-F

Use a comma to separate the conjunctive adverb from the rest of the sentence. (See page 151 for more information on conjunctive adverbs.)

Note: Some authors prefer to omit the comma after a short conjunctive adverb, e. g., thus, hence.

Example:

> The study of the Crusades is very interesting; <u>however</u>, it is also a very bloody time in history.

EXERCISE 1:

List five words which can be used as conjunctive adverbs. See lesson 20 B page 151 in *Learning English with the Bible,* if you need help.

1.

2.

3.

4.

5.

EXERCISE 2:

Underline the conjunctive adverbs in the following sentences and place a comma after the conjunctive adverb.

1. The eastern part of the Roman Empire was conquered by the Arabs; consequently Christians suffered.

2. Mohammed claimed to have received his thoughts from the angel Gabriel; nevertheless he did not believe in the God of the Bible.

3. Mohammed's teachings were recorded in the Koran; hence the Koran is the sacred book for Muslims.

4. Muslims believe that Mohammed is God's prophet; thus they do not accept Jesus Christ as God's Son.

5. Mecca is the birthplace of Mohammed; futhermore Mecca is the place where the sacred Kaaba is located.

6. Many Arabs did not like the teachings of Mohammed; therefore Mohammed left the city of Medina.

7. Mohammed died in A.D. 632; however his followers conquered North Africa, Spain and a part of France.

8. Islam might have conquered Europe; however the Christians defeated the Muslims at the battle of Tours.

9. Islam claims that followers who die in battle will gain rewards after death; hence the Muslims even today fight with courage.

10. Pilgrims to the Holy Land received bad treatment from the Turks; besides the Turks hated Christians.

LESSON 4-G

A comma is needed to separate introductory phrases from the rest of the sentence. Introductory phases may be prepositional phrases, participial phrases, infinitive phrases, or nominative absolutes.

Things to Remember:

1. A prepositional phrase consists of a preposition, a noun or pronoun following the preposition, and sometimes adjectives placed between the preposition and the noun.

   Example:

   > In Europe during the fourteenth and fifteenth centuries, the teaching of the Reformers flourished.

   Note: A simple introductory short prepositional phrase does not require a comma.

2. A participial phrase consists of a participle and its modifiers.

   Example:

   > Translating the Bible into English, John Wycliffe earned a place in Christian history.

3. An infinitive phrase consists of an infinitive plus modifier.

   Example:

   > To do well on a test, you must study.

4. A nominative absolute is a phrase consisting of a noun placed before a participial phrase.

Example:

John Huss having condemned indulgences, the Pope excommunicated him.

Note: When the participial phrase or the infinitive phrase is used as a subject of the sentence, no comma is needed.

Examples:

1. Understanding participial phrases is hard work.
2. To understand infinitives takes a little study.

EXERCISE 1:

Place commas where needed in the following sentences.

1. From around 476 to 1450 European history has been known as the Middle Ages.

2. Deprived of learning western Europe needed a revival.

3. Coming back from the Crusades men brought knowledge from other civilizations.

4. For the first time in centuries men began to desire new knowledge.

5. Writing about ancient civilizations became an important tool.

6. Living in a day of computers students cannot appreciate the laborious work of copying manuscripts.

7. During the time of the Renaissance a revival of learning occurred.

8. Money being supplied by patrons scholars began to investigate ancient documents.

9. In the Netherlands near Zwolle Thomas à Kempis lived.

10. Looking back into church history men discovered that a reform was needed in the church.

LESSON 4-H

A comma is needed to separate an introductory adverbial clause from the rest of the sentence.

Things to Remember:

1. A clause is a group of words with a subject and a verb, plus modifiers.

2. A complex sentence contains an independent clause and a dependent clause. (Dependent clauses begin with subordinating conjunctions. Example: since, if, because, when)

3. See pages 153–154 in *Learing English with the Bible* if you need help in understanding adverbial clauses.

   Example:

   > When men began to question certain practices in the church, the Reformation started.

EXERCISE 1:

List ten subordinating conjunctions (See page 154 in *Learning English with the Bible* if you have difficulty listing the subordinating conjunctions.)

1.

2.

3.

4.

5.

6.

7.

8.

9.

10.

EXERCISE 2:

Place a comma at the end of the adverbial clauses in the following sentences. Circle the subordinating conjunction. The first one has been done for you.

1. (Before) he became a monk, Martin Luther studied law.

2. Because Luther was concerned about his salvation he entered a monastery.

3. Since Luther felt doing good works would gain him salvation he practiced asceticism.

4. As he studied the Bible he read Romans 1:7.

5. When Luther realized his salvation depended on Christ alone he wrote the ninety-five theses.

6. After he nailed the ninety-five theses to the door of the Castle Church in Wittenberg his views became famous.

7. Although most professors used Latin in lecturing Luther taught in German.

8. In order that the common men could understand the Bible Luther translated the whole Bible.

9. Even though Luther is not famous for his hymns "A Mighty Fortress Is Our God" is well known.

10. Unless we know about the scholars who wrote during the Reformation our knowledge of church history is not complete.

TEST ON CHAPTER FOUR

Place commas wherever needed in the following sentences.

1. The Psalms a collection of praise and prayer is a book of poetry.

2. Needless to say David of course wrote many of the Psalms.

3. "Thou O Lord art a shield for me; . . ." (Ps. 3:3).

4. "Oh let the wickedness of the wicked come to an end, . . ." (Ps. 7:9).

5. "Selah" an expression used at the end of some Psalms could possibly mean a musical rest in chanting.

6. "Preserve me O God; for in thee do I put my trust" (Ps. 16:1).

7. Psalm 2 a Messianic Psalm tells of Christ as God's Son and King.

8. The imprecatory Psalms in my opinion might perplex many people.

9. "Behold how good and how pleasant it is for brethren to dwell together in unity" (Ps. 133:1).

10. "In the haughtiness of his countenance the wicked does not seek God" (Ps. 10:4).

11. "As silver tried in a furnace of the earth the words of the Lord are pure words" (Ps. 12:6).

12. We can learn much about God in the Psalms and then we should worship and adore Him.

13. When you finish reading a Psalm, record the theme of that Psalm.

14. To begin the day by reading the Bible is a beneficial exercise.

15. To behold the beauty of the Lord we must faithfully read His Word.

JUST FOR FUN

Listed below are eight lessons which we have studied for using the comma. See if you can find examples of each from a magazine or newspaper and insert the examples in the proper place. If you cannot find examples, then write your own.

LESSON 1

A comma is used to separate *nouns of direct address* from the rest of the sentence.

1.

2.

3.

4.

5.

LESSON 2

A comma is used to separate an *appositive* or an *appositional phrase* from the rest of the sentence. An *appositive* is a noun or noun phrase which follows a word and denotes or renames the same person, place, or thing.

1.

2.

3.

4.

5.

LESSON 3

A comma is used to separate *parenthetical expressions* from the rest of the sentence.

1.

2.

3.

4.

5.

LESSON 4

A comma is used to separate an interjection from the rest of the sentence.

1.

2.

3.

4.

5.

LESSON 5

Use a comma to separate independent clauses in a compound sentence. Remember, an independent clause is a simple sentence. The comma is placed before the coordinating conjunction.

1.

2.

3.

4.

5.

LESSON 6

Use a comma to separate the conjunctive adverb from the rest of the sentence.

1.

2.

3.

4.

5.

LESSON 7

A comma is needed to separate introductory phrases from the rest of the sentence. Introductory phrases may be prepositional phrases, participial phrases, infinitive phrases, or nominative absolutes.

1.

2.

3.

4.

5.

LESSON 8

A comma is needed to separate an introductory adverbial clause from the rest of the sentence.

1.

2.

3

4.

5.

JUST FOR FUN

1. Memorize a Psalm and tell your teacher about your effort.

2. Read an "Imprecatory Psalm," for example, Psalms 7, 35, 69, 139, and write a sentence telling the purpose of these Psalms.

Chapter 5

LEARNING ABOUT THE SEMICOLON

LESSON 5-A

A semicolon indicates a pause in a sentence. Place a semicolon between independent clauses in a compound sentence when no coordinating conjunction is used.

Example:

> God is doing marvelous things in our world; followers of Jesus Christ are increasing by hundreds every day.

Note: The two independent clauses in the above example could be made into two sentences by changing the semicolon to a period and placing a capital letter on the word "followers."

Example:

> God is doing marvelous things in our world. Followers of Jesus Christ are increasing by hundreds every day.

EXERCISE 1:

Place a semicolon between the two independent clauses in the following sentences:

1. The ultimate goal of God is to display his glory to all people the chief end of man is to glorify God and enjoy Him forever.

2. Find references in your Bible to terms like peoples, nations Gentiles remember not to think of these groups as countries.

3. Some statistics show that approximately 8,000 people groups have not been reached with the gospel about 16,000 groups are being taught the Word of God.

4. Unreached people are located in the interior of Irian Jaya other groups are living in ethnic neighborhoods in big cities.

5. Mission agencies have set goals to take the gospel to unreached people local churches are also reaching out to ethnic neighbors in their areas.

EXERCISE 2:

Write five compound sentences using semicolons between the independent clauses.

Example:

I enjoy holidays; my favorite is the Fourth of July.

1.

2.

3.

4.

5.

EXERCISE 3:

Write five compound sentences using coordinating conjunctions.

Example:

Doing exercises can be boring, but receiving rewards for accomplishment is great.

1.

2.

3.

4.

5.

EXERCISE 4:

Write five simple sentences using compound subjects. Underline the subjects.

Example:

<u>Boys</u> and <u>girls</u> prefer pizza to chopped liver.

1.

2.

3.

4.

5.

EXERCISE 5:

Write five simple sentences using compound verbs. Underline the verbs.

Example:

I <u>read</u> and <u>skate</u> in my free time.

1.

2.

3.

4.

5.

LESSON 5-B:

Place a semicolon before conjunctive adverbs which join independent clauses in a compound sentence.

Example:

> I studied conjunctive adverbs in a previous lesson; however, I need to look back for a listing of those words.

EXERCISE 1:

Place semicolons where needed in the following sentences. Underline the conjunctive adverbs. Be certain to place a comma after the conjunctive adverb.

Example:

> I know the need to send workers to unreached peoples; <u>therefore</u>, I want to be prepared to go.

1. The region between 10 to 40 degrees north of the equator contains 65% of the world's population nevertheless the area has 97% of the least evangelized countries of the earth.

2. The area contains 9 of the top ten worst countries regarding persecution thus Christians should pray for wisdom to reach these lands.

3. About 20% of all mission work is done in the 10/40 area consequently much work is needed.

4. Mission organizations are looking for people to go to lands in the 10/40 window moreover money is often available for sending Christians to these lands.

5. Christian workers to unreached people must be aware of the cultural differences however they must not compromise the Bible message.

Note: When the independent clauses are short, a comma or a period may take the place of a semicolon.

Examples:

> a.   I came, I saw, I conquered.
>
> b.   I came. I saw. I conquered.

LESSON 5-C:

Sometimes independent clauses in a compound sentence contain many commas, and to clarify it is necessary to use a semicolon to separate the clauses.

Example:

Hudson Taylor, one of the first missionaries to China, left England around 1854; but before he left, he worked for a physician to learn something about treating the sick.

TEST ON SEMICOLONS

Place semicolons or commas where needed in the following sentences.

1. Hudson Taylor's parents were Christians hence they were pleased that he wanted to go to China as a missionary.

2. He arrived in China during the Taiping Revolution but he was not injured in the uprising.

3. In the city of Shorphae in China he found friends with whom he could live.

4. Find out about the Taiping Revolution and write several facts.

5. Taylor wanted to marry another missionary Maria Dyer and he had to write her parents for permission.

6. It took about four months for a letter to reach England that seemed a long time to Taylor.

7. Taylor had strong moral values for example he believed Christians should stay out of debt.

8. He made many trips to inland China yet God protected him from harm.

9. Years later Taylor returned to England his visit resulted in the founding of the China Inland Misison.

10. Taylor and his wife returned to China they trusted God for their support.

JUST FOR FUN

Listed below are three lessons which we have studied for using semicolons. See if you can find examples of each from a magazine or newspaper and insert the examples in the proper place. If you cannot find examples, then write your own.

LESSON 1

A semicolon indicates a pause in a sentence. Place a semicolon between independent clauses in a compound sentence when no coordinating conjunction is used.

1.

2.

3.

4.

5.

LESSON 2

Place a semicolon before conjunctive adverbs which join independent clauses in a compund sentence.

1.

2.

3.

4.

5.

LESSON 3

Sometimes independent clauses in a compound sentence contain many commas; and to clarify, it is necessary to use a semicolon to separate the clauses.

1.

2.

3.

4.

5.

EXTRA CREDIT

Read about Hudson Taylor's life and discover what happened in China when he returned. Write a review of Taylor or of a missionary from your church.

Chapter 6

LEARNING ABOUT THE COLON

LESSON 6-A

Place a colon before a list of items, an enumeration, or a long quotation.

Examples:

1.   Have you read the following books: *Mere Christianity, The Chronicles of Narnia, David Copperfield?* (lists)

2.   In the colony of South Carolina, religious toleration was granted to all denominations: Calvinist, Huguenots, Episcopalians, Presbyterians, etc. (enumeration)

3.   The inscription on the Liberty Bell reads as follows: "And ye shall make hallow the fiftieth year, and proclaim liberty throughout the land unto all the inhabitants thereof; it shall be a jubilee."

Note: Punctuation before a listing of words varies with the length and form of the words which follow. For example, when <u>such as</u> introduces a short illustration, a comma may be used.

Example:

I would like to visit some historical sites, such as Gettysburg, the Alamo, and Bunker Hill.

LESSON 6-B

A colon may be placed after the salutation in a business letter.

Examples:

Dear Sir:

My dear Miss Smith:

LESSON 6-C

Use a colon between the parts of titles, references, and numerals.

Examples:

1.   *America: The Sorcerer's New Apprentice*

2.   Genesis 1:1

3.   8:30 AM

EXERCISE 1:

Tell why a colon is used in the following exercises:

1. Alexis de Tocqueville, a French statesman, related the following about America: "America is great because America is good, and if America ever ceases to be good, America will cease to be great."

_____

_____

_____

2. Gentlemen:

_____

3. Can you quote Proverbs 3:5, 6?

_____

4. For my camping trip I took the following: food, warm clothes, tenting equipment, and a camera.

_____

_____

5. Samuel Francis Smith wrote:

"My country 'tis of thee,
Sweet land of liberty,
Of thee I sing: . . ."

_____

_____

JUST FOR FUN

Listed below are the three lessons which we have studied on using the colon. See if you can find examples of each from a magazine or newspaper and insert the examples in the proper place. If you cannot find examples, then write your own.

LESSON 1

Place a colon before a list of items, an enumeration, or a long quotation.

1.

2.

3.

4.

5.

LESSON 2

A colon may be placed after the salutation in a business letter.

1.

2.

3.

4.

5.

LESSON 3

Use as colon between the parts of titles, references, and numerals.

1.

2.

3.

4.

5.

Chapter 7

LEARNING ABOUT THE HYPHEN

LESSON 7-A

Use a hyphen to indicate divisions of syllables of a word at the end of a sentence.

Example:

Francis Scott Key watched as the British freely, unmerci-
fully bombarded Fort McHenry.

LESSON 7-B

Use a hyphen to join parts of a compound word.

Note: Usage changes with the spelling of words. Check with a dictionary if you have doubts.

Examples:

a. off-color
b. passer-by

LESSON 7-C

Use a hyphen between the numerator and the denominator of a fraction.

Examples:

1. three-fourths
2. two-thirds

LESSON 7-D

Use a hyphen in compound numbers from twenty-one to ninety-nine.

LESSON 7-E

Use a hyphen between numerals and other words.

Examples:

a. thirty-hour week
b. fifty-mile run

LESSON 7-F

Sometimes a hyphen is used between a prefix and a word.

Examples:

   a.   pro-American

   b.   ex-president

TEST ON HYPHENS

Correct the following sentences. If no change is needed, write "correct" after the sentence.

1. Johann Kepler proved the helio-centric nature of the solar system.

2. The commander in chief is in charge of the armed forces.

3. Noah Webster completed his 26 year project of writing a dictionary in 1828.

4. Abraham Lincoln debated against Stephen Douglas's pro slavery bill.

5. Marcus Whitman, an American doctor and missionary, made a 3,000 mile trek east to persuade people to keep his mission.

6. Whitman's trek was in 1842-43.

7. James Wilson was one of six Founding Fathers to sign both the Declaration of Independence and the Constitution.

8. Rev. John Witherspoon reentered politics after his wife died.

9. King Ferdinand and Queen Isabella gave Columbus one tenth of the revenues he had been promised.

10. Vice President Calvin Coolidge became President after the death of President Harding.

JUST FOR FUN

Listed below are six lessons which we have studied for using the hyphen. See if you can find examples of each from a magazine or newspaper and insert the examples in the proper place. If you cannot find examples, then write your own.

LESSON 1

Use a hyphen to indicate divisions of syllables of a word at the end of a sentence.

1.

2.

3.

4.

5.

LESSON 2

Use a hyphen to join parts of a compound word.

1.

2.

3.

4.

5.

LESSON 3

Use a hyphen between the numerator and the denominator of a fraction.

1.

2.

3.

4.

5.

LESSON 4

Use a hyphen in compound numbers from twenty-one to ninety-nine.

1.

2.

3.

4.

5.

LESSON 5

Use a hyphen between numerals and other words.

1.

2.

3.

4.

5.

LESSON 6

Sometimes a hyphen is used between a prefix and a word.

1.

2.

3.

4.

5.

Chapter 8

LEARNING ABOUT THE DASH

A dash is usually the length of two hyphens.

Examples:

    a. hyphen –

    b. dash —

LESSON 8-A

A dash is used to denote a sudden break in thought.

Example:

    Did he—could he—get the paper written in time?

LESSON 8-B

A dash may be used to expand a phrase. Notice that an appositive is usually shorter than the phrase following a dash.

Example:

    Washington carefully planned each attack—a maneuver he hoped would end the war swiftly.

LESSON 8-C

A dash may be used before a summarizing phrase or clause that refers to nouns preceding the clause.

Example:

    Bach, Beethoven, and Brahms—all famous musicians who contributed much to our culture.

EXERCISE 1

Place a dash or dashes wherever needed in the following sentences.

1. Evolutionists claim to know everything about the missing link except where it is.

2. "Among which are life" the first inalienable right. (Henry Hyde)

3. "The character they portrayed was perfect, the character of a sinless Being One supremely wise and supremely good. . . . " (Simon Greenleaf)

4. "You who are here you, the educated and cultivated portion of the citizenship. . . . " (Giuseppe Garibaldi)

5. "I like to hear learned sermons and magnificent discourses appeals purely to the intellect abstract and abstruse ideas,. . . ." (Alfred Colquitt)

JUST FOR FUN

Listed below are 3 lessons which we have studied for using the dash. See if you can find examples of each from a magazine or newspaper and insert the examples in the proper place. If you cannot find examples, then write your own.

LESSON 1

A dash may be used to denote a sudden break in thought.

1.

2.

3.

4.

5.

LESSON 2

A dash may be used to expand a phrase.

1.

2.

3

4.

5.

LESSON 3

A dash may be used before a summarizing phrase or clause that refers to nouns preceding the clause.

1.

2.

3.

4.

5.

Chapter 9

LEARNING ABOUT CAPITALIZATION

Capitalization, as used today, is a rather recent technique.

See if you can find a book which is about a hundred years old. You will notice that the first capital letter is decorated and much larger in size. Sometimes Christmas cards use this large capital letter for the first word.

In addition, some authors capitalized all nouns just as the German language does today.

But times have changed. There are a few rules of capitalization that you should learn.

LESSON 9-A

Capitalize the first word in a sentence, a line of poetry, or a resolution.

Examples:

a. Do you know that Samuel Francis Smith wrote *My Country 'Tis of Thee?*

b. The fourth stanza begins:

"Our fathers' God to Thee,
Author of liberty,
To Thee we sing: . . ."

c. Be it resolved; That all students should learn the hymn.

EXERCISE 1

Place capital letters wherever needed in the following story.

one of the greatest chemists of all time was michael faraday. he pioneered the liquification of gasses. he also discovered benzene. this famous man wrote: the Christian who is taught by god finds his guide in the word of god.

EXERCISE 2

Write a poem of four lines; place capital letters where needed.

_____

_____

_____

_____

LESSON 9-B

Capitalize the first word in a title and all other words, except articles, conjunctions, and short prepositions.

Examples:

    a.   King Richard the Third

    b.   Let Us Have Faith

    c.   Idylls of the King

EXERCISE 1

Write the titles of five of your favorite books.

1.

2.

3.

4.

5.

LESSON 9-C

Capitalize the names of countries, states, cities, towns and the names of people who live there.

Examples:

    a. Japan

    b. Japanese

    c. Chattanooga, Tennessee

EXERCISE 1

Place capital letters wherever needed in the following sentences.

1. through his novel, *the scarlet letter*, nathaniel hawthorne became famous.

2. other well-known works of his include *the house of seven gables, twice-told tales*.

3. alexander solzhenitsyn, a famous russian author, was imprisoned by joseph stalin.

4. solzhenitsyn wrote *the gulag archipelago*.

5. if new yorkers live in the state of new york, what do you call people who live in michigan?

LESSON 9-D

Capitalize the letters "I and O." The word "oh" is not capitalized unless it is the first word in a sentence.

EXERCISE 1

Place capitals where needed in the following poem.

> *the star of calvary*
>
> by nathaniel hawthorne
>
> "behold, o israel, behold!
>   it is no human one.
> that you have dared to crucify.
>   what evil hath he done?
> it is your King, o israel,
>   the god-begotten Son."

LESSON 9-E

Capitalize the proper names, nicknames, titles, and initials of people.

Note: Capitalize names of relatives when they stand for the name of a person but never when preceded by a possessive pronoun.

Examples:

    a.   She is my mother.

    b.   Did Mother leave the house.

    c.   Booker T. Washington

EXERCISE 1

Place capital letters wherever needed in the following sentences. If the sentence is correct as written, write "correct" after it.

1. George washington was commander-in-chief of the army during the revolutionary war.

2. Washington was a descendant of king john of england.

3. When he was eleven years old, his father died.

4. Then he lived with his brother, augustine, in westmoreland county, virginia, near fredericksburg.

5. He attended william and mary college.

LESSON 9-F

Capitalize the names of buildings, ships, trains, planes, and documents, institutions and historical events.

Examples:

    World Trade Center

    Phoebe Snow (train)

    Battle of Waterloo

EXERCISE 1

Place capital letters wherever needed in the following sentences.

1. columbia university in new york city was originally called king's college.

2. The school was named after king george II.

3. Its seal consists of a seated woman and the hebrew tetragrammaton name of god, yhvh, written above her head.

4. The latin motto inscribed across the top reads: "in thy light we see light."

5. Christopher Columbus won the help of queen isabella of castile and king ferdinand of aragon to support his voyages.

6. Columbus's real name was cristobal colon.

7. His ships were called the santa maria, nina, and the pinta.

8. On the island of haiti, Columbus left forty men in a settlement named la navidad, meaning, "the nativity."

9. He encountered the cannibalistic tribe of the canibs, or caribs, from which caribbean originates.

10. In 1502 columbus, along with his brother, bartholomew, and son don ferdinand, explored the coasts of cuba, honduras, nicaragua, and costa rica.

LESSON 9-G

Capitalize the names of streets, locations, and regions. Do NOT capitalize directions (east, west, north, south) unless they indicate a region.

Examples:

Streets – Constitution Avenue

Cities – Oslo

Countries – Norway

Regions – Appalachian Mountains, the Northwest

EXERCISE 1

Capitalize words in the following sentences wherever necessary.

1. let's take a trip to europe and visit germany.

2. we shall depart on delta airline and arrive in frankfurt, a city in the southwest.

3. In the morning we'll embark on a cruise on the rhine river.

4. Our first stop will be at bonn, where beethoven was born.

5. We surely want to see king ludwig's fairy tale castle.

6. Soon we'll arrive at berlin, the capital and visit the brandenburg gate, the german state opera house, and the reichstag building.

7. Then we'll drive south to dresden, an historic city, and see the zwinger palace.

8. Of course, we'll want to visit oberammergau where the famous plays are held.

9. We must see lake constance and the black forest, near the dreisam river.

10. What a great trip, and oh, I would like to see the alps.

LESSON 9-H

Capitalize the months of the year, days of the week, and holidays. Do NOT capitalize the seasons.

EXERCISE 1:

1. In february we celebrate lincoln's and washington's birthdays.

2. In the spring some people have special church services on palm sunday and easter.

3. Others worship on maundy thursday and good friday.

4. On the last monday of may we usually observe memorial day.

5. On june 21, summer begins.

6. The autumnal equinox is on september 22.

7. The month of november contains election day, armistice day, and thanksgiving.

8. Thanksgiving occurs on the fourth thursday of november.

9. The season of winter, as well as other joyous holidays, arrives in december.

10. Do you know when columbus day is honored or passover or labor day?

LESSON 9-1

Capitalize names referring to the Bible, deity, holy books. Do NOT capitalize "god" or "gods" when referring to pagan gods.

Examples:
   a.   the Bible
   b.   our Father
   c.   Venus, or Roman god

EXERCISE 1

Place capital letters wherever needed in the following sentences.

1. The birth of jesus, the son of god, is recorded in matthew and mark.

2. Jesus is called the word in John 1:1.

3. The holy spirit is called the comforter in John 14.

4. In the magnificat (Luke 1:46–55) mary said that she rejoiced in god her savior.

5. John the baptist referred to jesus as the lamb of god.

6. The bible is very clear in stating that people should not worship pagan gods.

7. The pagan god of the phoenicians and canaanites was baal.

8. Other pagan gods mentioned in scripture are ashtoreth and molech.

9. Buddha founded buddhism; mohammed founded islam; jesus christ founded christianity.

10. Christians believe that only the bible is the word of god—not the koran or the talmud.

LESSON 9-J

Capitalize the names of specific subjects. If the subject has a number or letter after it, it should be capitalized. Do NOT capitalize the names of a general subject.

Example:

Typing 101; typing class

LESSON 9-K

Do NOT capitalize the names of classes unless it is a specific class.

Example:

junior; the Junior Class of Concord High School

LESSON 9-L

Capitalize names or initials which refer to political, racial, social, or civil groups.

Examples:

a. Negroes

b. House of Representatives

c. Awana Club

LESSON 9-M

Capitalize the first number in a hyphenated number. Do NOT capitalize the second word unless it is a proper noun.

Examples:

a. Forty-second Street

b. Franco-German

LESSON 9-N

Capitalize the brand names of products. Do NOT capitalize the product.

Example:

Palmolive soap

EXERCISE 1

Place capital letters wherever needed in the following sentences, or write "correct" if no capital letters are needed.

1. I enjoyed my senior year in high school the best.

2. The senior class of closter high school did many things.

3. We were allowed to study a variety of subjects, such as japanese I, fencing, calculus II, and animal life.

4. We traveled to detroit to see them manufacture trucks and ford automobiles.

5. In new york city we toured the metropolitan museum of art on eighty-second street and fifth avenue.

6. We observed a display of indian artifacts.

7. On our trip to the maxwell house factory, we were given free cups of coffee.

8. St. bartholomew's church, an episcopal church, on forty-ninth street has beautiful mosaics.

9. The cloisters, a medieval museum, has the tapestries depicting the unicorn.

10. The visit to the world trade center, the tallest building in new york, was very exciting.

REVIEW OF CAPITLIZATION

EXERCISE 1

Place capitals wherever needed in the following words or phrases.

1. abraham lincoln

2. president of the u.s.

3. the civil war

4. stephen a. douglas

5. southern states

6. the confederate army

7. fort sumter

8. general robert e. lee

9. appomattox, virginia

10. general ulysses s. grant

11. ford's theater

12. john wilkes booth

13. *illinois gazette*

14. independence hall

15. his inaugural address

16. supreme court case of dred scott v. sanford

17. chief justice roger b. taney

18. a chief justice

19. the battle

20. battle of bull run

21. a negro deputation

22. union troops

23. emancipation proclamation

24. the quakers

25. god, our father

26. his public address

27. gettysburg address

28. the white house

29. "that we here resolve . . . that this nation under god. . . ."

30. the lincoln memorial

JUST FOR FUN

Listed below are the fourteen lessons which we have studied on capitalization. See if you can find examples of each from a magazine or newspaper and insert the examples in the proper place. If you cannot find examples, then write your own.

LESSON 1

Capitalize the first word in a sentence, a line of poetry, or a resolution.

1.

2.

3.

4.

5.

LESSON 2

Capitalize the first word in a title and all other words, except articles, conjunctions, and short prepositions.

1.

2.

3.

4.

5.

LESSON 3

Capitalize the names of countries, states, cities, towns and the names of people who live there.

1.

2.

3.

4.

5.

LESSON 4

Capitalize the letter "I" and "O." The word "oh" is not capitalized unless it is the first word in a sentence.

1.

2.

3.

4.

5.

LESSON 5

Capitalize the proper names, nicknames, titles, and initials of people.

1.

2.

3.

4.

5.

LESSON 6

Capitalize the names of buildings, ships, trains, planes, documents, institutions, and historical events.

1.

2.

3.

4.

5.

LESSON 7

Capitalize the names of streets, locations, and regions. Do NOT capitalize directions (east, west, north, south) unless they indicate a region.

1.

2.

3.

4.

5.

LESSON 8

Capitalize the months of the year, days of the week, and holidays. Do NOT capitalize the seasons.

1.

2.

3.

4.

5.

LESSON 9

Capitalize names referring to the Bible, deity, holy books, Do NOT capitalize "god" or "gods" "when referring to pagan gods.

1.

2.

3.

4.

5.

LESSON 10

Capitalize the names of specific subjects. If the subject has a number or letter after it, it should be capitalized. Do NOT capitalize the names of a general subject.

1.

2.

3.

4.

5.

LESSON 11

Do NOT capitalize the names of classes unless it is a specific class.

1

2.

3.

4.

5.

LESSON 12

Capitalize names or initials which refer to political, racial, social, or civil groups.

1.

2.

3.

4.

5.

LESSON 13

Capitalize the first number in a hyphenated number. Do NOT capitalize the second word unless it is a proper noun.

1.

2.

3.

4.

5.

LESSON 14

Capitalize the brand names of products. Do NOT capitalize the product.

1.

2.

3.

4.

5.

Chapter 10

LEARNING ABOUT QUOTATIONS

To record the exact words that someone has said, you need to use quotation marks. Learn the rules of punctuation for using quotation marks.

LESSON 10-A

Use quotation marks to enclose a direct quotation.

Examples:

    A.   Andrew Johnson declared, "I do believe in Almighty God."

    B.   "I do believe in Almighty God," declared Andrew Johnson.

    C.   "Do you believe in Almighty God?" asked Andrew Jackson.

Note:

1. Notice that the exact words of the speaker are enclosed in quotation marks.

2. The first word of the speaker is always capitalized.

3. A comma follows the verb used by the speaker.

4. A period is always placed inside the quotation mark.

5. A comma is always placed inside the quotation mark.

6. If the quotation is a question or an exclamation, the question mark and exclamation point go inside the quotation mark.

EXERCISE 1

Punctuate the following sentences by using commas, periods, question marks, exclamation marks, and quotation marks.

1. Patrick Henry declared give me liberty or give me death

2. Was Patrick Henry a patriot asked the student

3. Alexis de Tocqueville proclaimed America is great because America is good, and it America ever ceases to be good, America will cease to be great

4. The New Testament is the very best book that ever was or ever will be known in the world remarked Charles Dickens

5. The historian asked was Alexis de Tocqueville French or English

6. Was John Adams a president requested Susan

7. Duty is ours; results are God's said John Quincy Adams

8. The teacher responded yes I agree

LESSON 10-B

An *indirect quotation* does not require quotation marks. In other words, when you tell what someone said without using the exact words of the speaker, do not use quotation marks.

Examples:
a. Direct quotation: Noah Webster stated, "Education is useless without the Bible."
b. Indirect quotation: Noah Webster stated that education is useless without the Bible.

EXERCISE 1

Supply capital letters and marks of punctuation in the following sentences.

1. abigail adams wrote the race is not to the swift, nor the battle to the strong

2. Abigail adams told her son John that he should sacrifice wealth and ease for defense of his country

3. In a letter to Thomas Jefferson, John Adams wrote the ten commandments and the sermon on the mount contain my religion

4. Did our second President, John Adams, believe that the Christian religion was a revelation asked the student

5. The inquisitive student will ask are John Adams and John Quincy Adams the same person

6. No, they are father and son replied the teacher

7. John Quincy Adams revealed his convictions and philosphy by saying that the only book deserving of universal attention is the Bible

8. John Quincy Adams wrote in his diary blessed, forever blessed, is the name of God

9. Who was Samuel Adams asked the history student

10. The teacher responded he was a cousin of John Adams

LESSON 10-C

When the name of the speaker is placed within a single spoken sentence, the second part of the words of the speaker begins with a small letter.

Examples:

    a. "The right to freedom," reported Samuel Adams, "is the gift of the Almighty."

    b. "All good moral philosophy," wrote Sir Francis Bacon, "is but the hand-maid to religion."

EXERCISE 1:

Supply capital letters and marks of punctuation where needed in the following sentences.

1. Who was George Bancroft asked Terry

2. The teacher told the class that Bancroft directed the establishment of the U.S. Naval Academy at Annapolis.

3. Oh I would like to attend that college remarked Terry

4. You may if you study hard

5. Did Commodore Perry asked Terry attend Annapolis

6. Then the teacher asked the class did you know that Samuel Pepys, the British author, was in the British Navy

7. Must I go to Annapolis to be in the navy asked Terry.

8. The teacher responded of course not

9. Well replied the student my ambition is to be an astronaut.

10. That's great answered the teacher because you are a fine student

LESSON 10-D

When the name of the speaker is placed between two sentences, the second sentence begins with a capital letter.

Examples:

a. "Did you know that Katherine Lee Bates wrote *America the Beautiful?*" asked the teacher. "Do you know that song?"

b. "Yes, I know that patriotic hymn," responded Betty. "It's a lovely song."

EXERCISE 1

Supply capital letters and marks of punctuation where needed.

1. Henry Ward Beecher was an abolitionist said the teacher he wrote *Uncle Tom's Cabin*

2. Did you know that 74% of our Founding Father's quotes were derived from the bible

3. Frank Borman was the commander of Apollo VIII spoke the student that spacecraft was the first manned ship to orbit the moon.

4. Did the colonists disguise themselves as Indians queried the teacher when they threw the tea in the Boston Harbor

5. Yes, I know that responded Bob did that occur in 1773 or 1774

6. Where did the name "Minutemen" come from asked Stephanie were they well-trained

7. No answered the teacher

8. the Pilgrims left Holland reported the orator in 1620

9. Didn't they live in England before they lived in Holland asked Joel

10. Yes they did replied the teacher they left England because of religious persecution

LESSON 10-E

Place quotation marks around titles of short stories, essays, one-act plays, chapters in a book, magazine articles, songs, and poems.

Examples:

    a.   Most children learn the poem "Jack and Jill."

    b.   One of my favorite short stories is "The Necklace."

LESSON 10-F

Titles of newspapers, magazines, books, or plays are italicized. If they are handwritten or typed, they should be underlined.

EXERCISE 1

Place quotation marks or underlines where needed in the following sentences.

1. Historical novels, such as a tale of two cities and johnny tremain, make fascinating reading.

2. The raven a poem by poe is easy to memorize.

3. The new york times is read worldwide.

4. Christianity Today and moody monthly are well-known magazines.

5. A song frequently used at weddings is the lord's prayer.

6. Do you know who wrote little women?

7. Thomas Paine's famous essay was entitled common sense.

8. Missionary Travels and Researches in South Africa is a work by David Livingston.

9. Henry Morton Stanley was a correspondent for the new york herald.

10. Rush Limbaugh, who hosts a radio show, authored The Way Things Ought to Be.

LESSON 10-G

A quotation that appears inside a quoted sentence needs single quotation marks.

Example:

"Did Jesus say, 'I am the way, the truth, and the life'?" asked the Sunday School teacher.

LESSON 10-H

Quotation marks are placed at the beginning and end of a quotation containing several sentences. Each sentence within the quotation does not need quotation marks.

Example:

The teacher asked, "Was John Brown an abolitionist? Did he open his barn in Pennsylvania as a station on the Underground Railroad?"

LESSON 10-I

Begin a new paragraph whenever two or more people are having a conversation.

Example:

One historian said, "George Washington Carver introduced hundreds of uses for the peanut, soybeans, pecan and sweet potato."

Another writer wrote, "Carver was raised by his uncle and aunt."

REVIEW ON QUOTATIONS AND ITALICS

EXERCISE 1

Punctuate the following sentences.

1. Samuel Taylor Coleridge, an English poet, wrote The Rime of the Ancient Mariner.

2. He is reported to have said I know the Bible is inspired because it finds me at greater depths of my being than any other book.

3. Eric said I like the lines that say He prayeth best who loveth best.

4. A favorite exam question is what was the site of the first Continental Congress?

5. Calvin Coolidge, when speaking of the motives of the Puritans, said They were intent upon establishing a Christian commonwealth.

6. Someone asked me do you know what document contains when in the course of human events

7. The novel Robinson Crusoe has been made into a movie.

8. The New Testament remarked Charles Dickens is the very best book that was ever written.

9. John Dickinson wrote a series of essays called Fabius.

10. Was Frederick Douglass a slave who became a spokesman for all slaves asked Dale.

JUST FOR FUN

Listed below are the nine lessons which we have studied on using quotations. See if you can find examples of each from a magazine or newspaper and insert the examples in the proper place. If you cannot find examples, then write your own.

LESSON 1

Use quotation marks to enclose *a direct quotation.*

1.

2.

3.

4.

5.

LESSON 2

An *indirect quotation* does not require quotation marks. In other words, when you tell what someone said without using the exact words of the speaker, do not use quotation marks.

1.

2.

3.

4.

5.

LESSON 3

When the name of the speaker is placed within a single spoken sentence, the second part of the words of the speaker begins with a small letter.

1.

2.

3.

4.

5.

LESSON 4

When the name of the speaker is placed between two sentences, the second sentence begins with a capital letter.

1.

2.

3.

4.

5.

LESSON 5

Place quotation marks around titles of short stories, essays, one-act plays, chapters in a book, magazine articles, songs, and poems.

1.

2

3.

4.

5.

LESSON 6

Titles of newspapers, magazines, books, or plays are italicized. If they are handwritten or typed, they should be underlined.

1.

2.

3

4.

5.

LESSON 7

A quotation that appears inside a quoted sentence needs single quotation marks.

1.

2.

3.

4.

5.

LESSON 8

Quotation marks are placed at the beginning and end of a quotation containing several sentences. Each sentence within the quotation does not need quotation marks.

1.

2.

3.

4.

5.

LESSON 9

Begin a new paragraph whenever two or more people are having a conversation.

1.

2.

3.

4.

5.

FINAL TEST ON PUNCTUATION AND CAPITALIZATION

Place capital letters, end marks, quotation marks, semicolons, commas, colons, hyphens, and dashes where needed in the following sentences.

1. Has archaeology confirmed the accuracy of many bible stories asked the teacher have records of places and people been discovered

2. Even though scripture does not give the exact location of the garden of eden scientists have given geographical evidence for its location

3. In genesis 2 there is a reference to a river called hiddekél the ancient name for the tigris river

4. Somewhere in the tigris euphrates valley in the area of mesopotamia was the garden of eden

5. Professor w f albright a well known archeologist studied cuneiforms.

6. Some believe moses found clay tablets and he then edited them and wrote the pentateuch the first five books of the bible.

7. Could men actually have lived for hundreds of years as seen in the sumerian king list

8. The book of the dead is a volume dealing with life in ancient egypt and suggests that egyptians were polytheistic.

9. Students did you ever hear of nimrod the mighty hunter

10. At nineveh in ancient assyria a statue of nimrod was excavated

11. Do you believe in a recent creation of the world thousands of years rather than millions of years

12. The dead sea scrolls were discovered in a cave at qumran and a part of them was taken to the american school of oriental research at jerusalem.

13. Because many artifacts which are mentioned have been found higher critics have had to reevaluate their claims

14. To analyze broken pieces of pottery called ostraca is a difficult task

15. Analyzing broken pieces of pottery archeologists discovered many facts

16. Fragments of new testament papyri the John Rylands Fragment the Chester Beatty Papyri and the Bodmer Papyri confirm the dates of composition for some books of the bible.

17. Biblical writers used stone as writing material this fact is proven by discoveries of the code of hammurabi the rosetta stone and the moabite stone

18. As early as october 2 1515 Desiderius Erasmus of Rotterdam the dutch scholar and humanist printed the first greek new testament and this later became the basis for the so-called textus receptus

19. Now exclaimed the teacher wouldn't you like to be an archeologist? You would discover many interesting facts about the life of early people.

20. After studying all the information in this book, said the student, I feel I have the patience to study to be an archeologist

ANSWERS

Chapter 1

LESSON 1-A

EXERCISE 1

  1. ?   interrogative

  2. . or ! exclamatory

  3. .   declarative

  4. .   imperative

  5. ?   interrogative

  6. .   declarative

  7. ?   interrogative

  8. .   declarative

  9. . or ! elliptical

  10. . or ! exclamatory

EXERCISE 2 Teacher to correct

EXERCISE 3 Teacher to correct

EXERCISE 4 Teacher to correct

EXERCISE 5 Teacher to correct

EXERCISE 6 Teacher to correct

ANSWERS

Chapter 2

EXERCISE 1:

1. Mr.   A.D.   1868.

2. 1835.

3. College?

4. ft.   in.   mind.

5. minute.

6. Wow!

7. Land.   visit.

EXERCISE 2:

2. 8

3. 1

4. 2

5. 10

6. 9

7. 4

8. 3

9. 5

10. 7

11. 15

12. 13

13. 11

14. 12

15. 14

EXERCISE 3:

1. Has been done for you.

2. Maine

3. Iowa

4. Massachusetts

5. Washington

6. Alaska

7. Arizona

8. Wisconsin

9. Delware

10. Maryland

EXERCISE 4

1. namely

2. Doctor of Laws

3. noun

4. adjective

5. synonym

6. verb transitive

7. Latin

8. plural

9. pages

10. French

ANSWERS

Chapter 3

LESSON 3-A

EXERCISE 1:

1. and

2. but

3. or

4. nor

5. for

6. so

7. yet

EXERCISE 2:

1. emperor, martyr,

2. captured, scourged,

3. Decius, Aurelius,

4. sick, torments, prayer,

5. martyred, destroyed,

6. passageways, catacombs,

7. prayed, sang,

8. Origen, Blandina,

9. salvation, joy,

10. stake, beasts,

LESSON 3-C

EXERCISE 1:

1. Clement, Ignatius,

2. no comma needed

3. simple,

4. no comma needed

5. hard, laborious,

6. no comma needed

7. creeds, canons,

8. Creed, Creed,

9. no comma needed

10. "presbyter," "bishop," "diocese,"

Test on Chapter 3

1. B.C.

2. religious, political, Bible?

3. Noah, wife, came.

4. love ! or .

5. land.

6. B.C.

7. after ending parenthesis mark

8. years.).

9 Pharisees, Sadducees, and Koran?

10. 6, A. D. 70, Jerusalem.

ANSWERS

Chapter 4

LESSON 4-A

EXERCISE 1:

1. <u>Mr. Server,</u>

2. I, <u>my friend</u>

3. now, <u>John,</u>

4. <u>Goosey</u>, <u>Goosey</u>, <u>Gander,</u>

5. Students,

6. listen, <u>my children,</u>

7. Hence, <u>loathed Melancholy</u>

8. thee, <u>ruthless King</u>

9. Return, <u>O, holy Dove,</u>

10. <u>Little Lamb</u>,

LESSON 4-B

EXERCISE 1:

1. Fathers, <u>Ambrose</u>, <u>Jerome</u>, <u>Augustine,</u>

2. Jerome, <u>another great leader in the church,</u>

3. Bible, <u>the Vulgate,</u>

4. Fathers, <u>Augustine,</u>

5. Monica, <u>Augustine's mother</u>,

6. works, <u>Confessions</u> and <u>The City of God.</u>

7. pillar, <u>a stylus</u>

8. Chrysostom, <u>an eloquent preacher,</u>

9. houses, <u>monasteries</u>

10. God, <u>the Bible</u>,

EXERCISE 2: TEACHER TO CORRECT

LESSON 4-C

EXERCISE 1

1. Teacher to decide

2. Teacher to decide

3. Teacher to decide

4. Teacher to decide

5. Teacher to decide

EXERCISE 2

1. <u>,of course</u>,

2. and, <u>therefore</u>,

3. <u>To be sure</u>,

4. Bible, <u>moreover</u>,

5. <u>Futhermore</u>,

6. means, <u>in other words,</u>

7. fossils, <u>for example,</u>

8. <u>For example,</u>

9. do, <u>however,</u>

10. <u>Needless to say,</u>

LESSON 4-D

1. <u>Well,</u>

2. <u>Wow,</u>

3. <u>Oh,</u>

4. <u>Hurrah,</u>

5. <u>Ah,</u>

LESSON 4-E

EXERCISE 1

1. and

2. or

3. nor

4. for

5. but

6. yet

7. so

EXERCISE 2

1. ,but

2. uncivilized, yet

3. interesting, for

4. king, and

5. monk, or

6. Christianity, for

7. Germany, and

8. names, and

9. Christianity, yet

10. Europe, and

LESSON 4-F

EXERCISE 1

1. nevertheless

2. however

3. consequently

4. therefore

5. indeed

Teacher should accept other conjunctive adverbs.

EXERCISE 2

1. <u>consequently</u>,

2. <u>nevertheless</u>,

3. <u>hence</u>,

4. <u>thus</u>,

5. <u>furthermore</u>,

6. <u>therefore</u>,

7. <u>however</u>,

8. <u>however</u>,

9. <u>hence</u>,

10. <u>besides</u>,

LESSON 4-G

EXERCISE 1

1. 1450,

2. learning,

3. Crusades,

4. centuries,

5. none needed

6. computers,

7. Renaissance,

8. patrons,

9. Zwolle,

10. history,

LESSON 4-H

EXERCISE 1

1. when

2. because

3. since

4. if

5. as

6. although

7. before

8. after

9. unless

10. while

Teachers may accept other subordinating conjuctions.

EXERCISE 2

1. Has been done for you.

2. (Because) salvation,

3. (Since) salvation,

4. (As) Bible,

5. (When) alone,

6. (After) Wittenberg,

7. (Although) lecturing,

8. (In order that) Bible,

9. (Even though) hymns,

10. (Unless) Reformation,

Test on Chapter Four

1. Psalms, prayer,

2. Needless to say, David, course,

3. Thou, Lord,

4. Oh,

5. "Selah," Psalms,

6. me,

7. 2, Psalm,

8. Psalms, opinion,

9. Behold,

10. countenance,

11. earth,

12. Psalms,

13. Psalm,

14. none needed

15. Lord,

ANSWERS

Chapter 5

LESSON 5-A

EXERCISE 1

1. people;

2. Gentiles;

3. gospel;

4. Jaya;

5. people;

EXERCISE 2

Teacher to correct

EXERCISE 3

Teacher to correct

EXERCISE 4

Teacher to correct

EXERCISE 5

Teacher to correct

LESSON 5-B

EXERCISE 1

1. population; <u>nevertheless</u>,

2. persecution; <u>thus</u>,

3. area; <u>consequently,</u>

4. window; <u>moreover,</u>

5. differences; <u>however,</u>

Test on Semicolons

1. Christians; hence,

2. Revolution,

3. China,

4. none needed

5. missionary, Dyer,

6. England;

7. values; example,

8. China,

9. England;

10. China;

ANSWERS

Chapter 6

EXERCISE 1

1. A colon is needed before a long quotation.

2. A colon is needed after the salutation in a business letter.

3. A colon is placed between numerals.

4. A colon is used before lists.

5. A colon is needed before a long quotation.

ANSWERS

Chapter 7

Test on Hyphens

1. heliocentric

2. commander-in-chief

3. 26-year

4. pro-slavery

5. 3,000-mile

6. correct

7. correct

8. correct—re-entered is also acceptable

9. one-tenth

10. Vice-

ANSWERS

Chapter 8

Test on Dashes

1. link—

2. life—

3. Being—

4. here—

5. discourses—intellect—

ANSWERS

Chapter 9

LESSON 9-A

EXERCISE 1

1. One . . .

2. Michael Faraday . . .

3. He . . .

4. He . . .

5. This . . .

6. The . . .

7. God . . .

8. Word of God . . .

EXERCISE 2

Teacher to correct

LESSON 9-A

EXERCISE 1

Teacher to correct

LESSON 9-C

1. Through . . . *The Scarlet Letter*, Nathaniel Hawthorne

2. Other, *The House of Seven Gables, Twice–Told Tales.*

3. Alexander Solzhenitsyn, Russian, Joseph Stalin.

4. Solzhenitsyn, *The Gulag Archipelago.*

5. If, New Yorkers,   New York,   Michigan

LESSON 9-D

1. The Star of Calvary

   Nathaniel Hawthorne

2. Behold, O Israel

   It, One

3. That

   What, He

4. It, O Israel

   The God

LESSON 9-E

1. Washington, Commander, Chief, Revolutionary War

2. King John, England

3. correct

4. Augustine, Westmoreland County,

   Virginia, Fredericksburg

5. William, Mary College

LESSON 9-F

1. Columbia University, New York City, King's College

2. King George

3. Hebrew, Tetragrammaton, God, YHVH,

4. Latin, In, Thy,

5. Queen, Isabella, Castile, King Ferdinand, Aragon

6. Cristobal Colon

7. Santa Maria, Nina, Pinta

8. Haiti, La Navidad, The Nativity

9. Canibs, Caribs, Caribbean

10. Columbus, Bartholomew, Don Ferdinand

    Cuba, Honduras, Nicaragua, Costa Rica

LESSON 9-G
EXERCISE 1

1. Let's, Europe, Germany

2. We Delta Airline, Frankfurt, Southwest

3. Rhine River

4. Bonn, Beethoven

5. King Ludwig's

6. Berlin, Brandenburg Gate, German State Opera House, Reichstag Building

7. Dresden, Zwinger Palace

8. Oberammergau

9. Lake Constance, Black Forest, Dreisam River

10. Alps

LESSON 9-H

1. February, Lincoln's and Washington's

2. Palm Sunday, Easter

3. Maundy Thursday, Good Friday

4. Monday, May, Memorial Day

5. June

6. September

7. November, Election Day, Armistice Day, Thanksgiving

8. Thursday, November

9. December

10. Columbus Day, Passover, Labor Day

LESSON 9-I
EXERCISE 1

1. Jesus, Son, God, Matthew, Mark

2. Word

3. Holy Spirit, Comforter

4. Magnificat, Mary, God, Savior

5. Baptist, Jesus, Lamb, God

6. Bible

7. Phoenicians, Canaanites, Baal

8. Scripture, Ashtoreth, Molech

9. Buddhism, Mohammed, Islam, Jesus Christ, Christianity

10. Bible, Word, God, Koran, Talmud

LESSON 9-N
EXERCISE 1

1. correct

2. Senior Class, Closter High School

3. Japanese I, Calculus II

4. Detroit, Ford

5. New York City, Metropolitan Museum of Art, Eighty, Street, Fifth Avenue

6. Indian

7. Maxwell House

8. Bartholomew's Church, Episcopal, Forty

9. Cloisters, Unicorn

10. World Trade Center, New York

Review of Capitalization

Exercise 1

1. Abraham Lincoln

2. President, U.S.

3. Civil War

4. Stephen A. Douglas

5. none needed

6. Confederate Army

7. Fort Sumter

8. General Robert E. Lee

9. Appomattox, Virginia

10. General Ulysses S. Grant

11. Ford's Theater

12. John Wilkes Booth

13. Illinois Gazette

14. Independence Hall

15. Inaugural Address

16. Supreme Court, Dred Scott, Sanford

17. Chief Justice Roger B. Taney

18. none needed

19. none needed

20. Battle Bull Run

21. Negro

22. Union

23. Emancipation Proclamation

24. Quakers

25. God, Father

26. none needed

27. Gettysburg Address

28. White House

29. That, God

30. Lincoln Memorial

ANSWERS

Chapter 10

LESSON 10-A

EXERCISE 1

1. declared, "Give . . . death."

2. "Was . . . patriot?" asked the student.

3. proclaimed, "America . . . great."

4. "The . . . world," Dickens.

5. asked, "Was . . . English?"

6. "Was . . . president?" Susan.

7. "Duty . . . God's,"

8. responded, "Yes . . . agree."

LESSON 10-B

EXERCISE 1

1. Abigail Adams wrote, "The . . . strong."

2. Adams . . . country.

3. wrote, "The Ten Commandments . . . Sermon Mount . . . religion."

4. "Did . . . revelation?" . . . student.

5. ask, "Are . . . person?"

6. "No, . . . son," teacher.

7. Bible.

8. diary, "Blessed . . . God."

9. "Who . . . Adams?" student.

10. responded, "He . . . Adams."

LESSON 10-C

EXERCISE 1

1. "Who . . . Bancroft?" asked Terry.

2. none needed

3. "Oh, . . . college," remarked Terry.

4. hard.

5. "Did . . . Perry," asked Terry, "attend Annapolis?"

6. class, "Did . . . Navy?"

7. "Must . . . navy?"

8. responded, "Of course not."

9. "Well," replied the student, "my . . . astronaut."

10. "That's great," answered the teacher, "because . . . student."

LESSON 10-D

EXERCISE 1

1. "Henry . . . abolitionist," said the teacher. "He . . . *Cabin*."

2. Bible?

3. "Frank . . . VIII," spoke the student. "That . . . moon."

4. "Did . . . Indians," queried the teacher, "when . . . Harbor?"

5. "Yes . . . that," responded Bob. "Did . . . 1774?"

6. "Where . . . from?" asked Stephanie. "Were . . . well-trained?"

7. "No," answered the teacher.

8. "The . . . Holland," . . . 1620.

9. "Didn't . . . Holland?" asked Joel.

10. "Yes, they did," replied the teacher. "They . . . persecution."

LESSON 10-F

EXERCISE 1

1. A Tale of Two Cities and Johnny Tremain

2. "The Raven," . . . Poe,

3. New York Times

4. Christianity Today and Moody Monthly

5. "The Lord's Prayer."

6. Little Women?

7. "Common Sense."

8. Missionary Travels and Researches in South Africa

9. New York Herald.

10. The Way Things Ought to Be.

Review on Quotations and Italics

1. Samuel Taylor Coleridge, an English poet, wrote "The Rime of the Ancient Mariner."

2. He is reported to have said, "I know the Bible is inspired because it finds me at greater depths of my being than any other book."

3. Eric said, "I like the lines that say, 'He prayeth best who loveth best.'"

4. A favorite exam question is, "What is the site of the first Continental Congress?"

5. Calvin Coolidge, when speaking of the motives of the Puritans, said, "They were intent upon establishing a Christian commonwealth."

6. Someone asked me, "Do you know what document contains 'when, in the course of human events'?"

7. The novel <u>Robinson Crusoe</u> has been made into a movie.

8. "The New Testament," remarked Charles Dickens, "is the very best book that was ever written."

9. John Dickinson wrote a series of essays called "Fabius."

10. "Was Frederick Douglass a slave who became a spokesman for all slaves?" asked Dale.

Final Test Answers

1. "Has archaeology confirmed the accuracy of many Bible stories?" asked the teacher. "Have records of places and people been discovered?"

2. Even though Scripture does not give the exact location of the Garden of Eden, scientists have given geographical evidence for its location.

3. In Genesis 2 there is a reference to a river called Hiddekél, the ancient name for the Tigris River.

4. Somewhere in the Tigris Euphrates valley in the area of Mesopotamia was the Garden of Eden. **A dash is acceptable between the words "valley" and "in"**

5. Professor W. F. Albright, a well-known archeologist, studied cuneiforms.

6. Some believe Moses found clay tablets, and he then edited them and wrote the Pentateuch, the first five books of the Bible.

7. Could men actually have lived for hundreds of years as seen in the Sumerian king list?

8. The Book of the Dead is a volume dealing with life in ancient Egypt and suggests that Egyptians were polytheistic.

9. Students, did you ever hear of Nimrod, the mighty hunter?

10. At Nineveh in ancient Assyria, a statue of Nimrod was excavated.

11. Do you believe in a recent creation of the world—thousand of years rather than millions of years?

12. The Dead Sea Scrolls were discovered in a cave at Qumran, and a part of them was taken to the American School of Oriental Research at Jerusalem.

13. Because many artifacts which are mentioned have been found, higher critics have had to reevaluate their claims.

14. To analyze broken pieces of pottery, called ostraca, is a difficult task.

15. Analyzing broken pieces of pottery, archeologists discovered many facts.

16. Fragments of New Testament papyri—the John Rylands Fragment, the Chester Beatty Papyri, and the Bodmer Papyri—confirm the dates of composition for some books of the Bible.

17. Biblical writers used stone as writing material; this fact is proven by discoveries of the Code of Hammurabi, the Rosetta Stone, and the Moabite Stone.

    OR

    Biblical writers used stone as writing material. This

18. As early as October 2, 1515, Desiderius Erasmus of Rotterdam, the Dutch scholar and humanist, printed the first Greek New Testament, and this later became the basis for the so-called Textus Receptus.

19. "Now," exclaimed the teacher, "wouldn't you like to be an archeologist? You would discover many interesting facts about the life of early people."

20. "After studying all the information in this book," said the student, "I feel I have the patience to study to be an archeologist."